Father-Son Ministry

1 Corinthians 4:15

Reassessing Apostolic and Prophetic Perspectives

Dr. Stephen R. Crosby
Stephanos Ministries

Introduction

The practical value of what we believe is proven in implementation. Faith that saves is a living thing, and in the living of our faith, its value is truly seen. If our faith translates inaccurately into how we live, then what we believe may save our souls, but our testimony is compromised and His kingdom advance hindered. If our faith is not incarnate, others have a legitimate right to question our beliefs. Jesus said it this way: "You will know them by their fruits."

Accurate thought expressed inaccurately has consequences. Legitimate biblical concepts held in an unhealed heart, implemented with unclean hands, propagated with crooked feet, and expressed beyond legitimate boundaries, are ruined. That which is intended for good ends up causing harm.

The concept of spiritual fathers and sons[1] fits the above categorization. It's a legitimate biblical concept and it has associated benefits and risks. The problem is not in the belief per se. It's in the expression. It's my conviction from the Scriptures, as well as from subjective observation, that the f/s paradigm, as it is widely believed and practiced, needs some adjustment. In some cases, it just needs a tune up. In other cases, the wheels are off the bus and the engine is throwing piston rods.

A scalpel's potential for benefit or harm is entirely in the hands of the surgeon. Properly trained and gifted surgeons maximize benefit and minimize risk, even when pain is inevitably part of the process. The f/s scalpel is not bad, and pain is always part of the process. However, some of the hands implementing the f/s scalpel are a bit shaky and there's arterial bleeding in the Body of Christ. The f/s idea needs to be implemented with the spiritual equivalent of surgical skill to avoid traumatizing the Body of Christ with good intentions.

The f/s ministry paradigm also has very specific, biblically designed-for-life, boundaries of expression that are routinely violated by the well-meaning misinformed, the unhealed insecure, and propagandists with a personal agenda.

---

[1]1 Corinthians 4:15 et al., - no gender specificity is implied in these terms, hereafter abbreviated f/s.

I realize that this effort might be relevant to only a small segment of a small segment of the Body of Christ. Most believe apostles and prophets do not exist today. Many have no exposure to the "father-son" paradigm of ministry. They will have little to no understanding of what I am talking about. Others might theoretically believe in these things, but have little or no practical experience. Others might have experience but they've not run into some of the issues I address herein (If you have any tenure at all within so-called "apostolic and prophetic" environments, and if honesty prevailed, I would doubt it).

These folks might think I'm too negative, that I'm throwing the baby out with the bath water, and that I can only see the things that are wrong, that things "aren't that bad," that their experience in spiritual parenting has been great, and so on. I would respond to you that just because you've not experienced what I have does not negate my experience. You do not receive the emails that I do from around the world. I receive testimony after testimony of chaos and abuse that leaves lives in ruin. God cares about these folks and wants them set free, healed, and restored.

If these issues don't apply to you, rejoice! You've been blessedly protected. However, thousands of others have not been so fortunate. The things I am writing about are epidemic and considered normative within apostolic and prophetic circles. Variations on these themes are common elsewhere. I pray that the content herein ***will never be useful to you***. Nothing would make me happier. But the day may come for you, or for someone you know, that this material's relevance could significantly change.

Part I herein examines thirteen areas in which the f/s ministry paradigm is being implemented poorly, exceeding legitimate biblical boundaries, or careening into falsehood and abuse. Part II discusses some unique elements of the relationship between apostles and prophets that intersect the "father-son" ministry issue.

Part I

Trash and Treasure

The theme of family saturates Scripture. The shared covenantal love in the Godhead is to be reflected on earth through natural and spiritual family relationships. The language, spirit, and methods of family are kingdom normal. However, the cults use the principle of family with great effect to win people into their association and to establish unbiblical belief systems and practices. Even the idea of family can be pushed too far.[2]

Just advocating for family, natural or spiritual, is not enough. Our advocacy must be within biblical boundaries and Holy Spirit insight. Whatever we might believe to be a legitimate expression of family, (spiritual or natural), it must be sustained by more than select proof texts and verses quoted and applied out of context (an epidemic problem).

Any "thing" born of the Spirit, sustained by the Spirit, and implemented in love is wonderful. This includes the concept of spiritual parenting (f/s – father/sons). The very same thing when humanly contrived is ugly and will result in the aberrations I will herein describe. Without diligence in definition and practice kingdom normal can become quite distorted and cause great human pain. This essay is not about winning a theological point. It's about minimizing pain.

We know that our adversary will always ally with our carnality to ruin any "God-thing." The devil is good at deviling. In the matter of spiritual parenting, his garbage cart has been throwing a lot of doctrinal and methodological filth into the field of the Lord. Our carnality has been picking it up and bronzing it.

It's going to be necessary to dig through a lot of trash and avoid a lot of pitfalls if we are to find the treasure of kingdom increase in the reality of Spirit-birthed and Spirit-wrought relationships. If we believe in the value of the treasure, we will plug our noses, put on our boots, and wade through the waste.

---

[2] E.g. – The LatterDay Saints/Mormonism.

I hope by shining light on various corruptions and pitfalls that the treasure hunt will be easier for others than it was for me. The good news is - I've shoveled a ton of garbage, climbed out of a few pits, and found the treasure. I am enjoying the best relational days of my life. Trash is becoming a memory.

Limitations and Pitfalls to Avoid

What, if any, are the biblical limitations or problems associated with the language and methodology of spiritual parenting (father/sons-f/s) as it is commonly expressed in apostolic and prophetic circles?

1. The Limitation of Family #1 – Spiritual Metaphor

The Scriptures refer to believers in churches as children in several passages such as: 2 Corinthians 6:13, 12:14; 1 Thessalonians 2:7, 2:11; Galatians 4:19; 1 Peter 1:14, and multiple times in John's epistles. The Corinthian and Galatian passages use children as a metaphor for their state of spiritual infancy. It's not necessarily a compliment, model, or standard be maintained for all time. It is a metaphor for a season of spiritual development that we pass through onto maturity.[3]

The Thessalonian verses also use the term as a metaphor for Paul's tenderness and affections among them. First Peter 1:14–15 also uses it as a metaphor for the believer's relationship to God, **not** their relationship to leaders[4] or mentors. In John's epistles, it is again a metaphor describing John's affection/heart state toward them, especially in their spiritual infancy.

Paul explicitly refers to only three people as his sons: Onesimus, Timothy, and Titus.[5] In each case Paul applied the term to those for whom he was instrumental in their conversion process and subsequent development. Peter refers to Mark as his son once in 1 Peter 5:13. Paul refers to himself generically as a father in 1 Corinthians 4:15:

---

[3] 1 John - little children, young men, fathers.

[4] I am not a fan of the term "leader." It has some cultural baggage associated with it that is nearly insurmountable to overcome and the NT Scripture does not use it specifically. I much prefer "follower" to leader as in the Pauline: "Follow me as I follow the Lord." In that sense, yes, it is leadership.

[5] Philemon 10; 2 Timothy 2:1; Titus 1:4.

For though you have ten thousand instructors in Christ,
you have not many fathers;
for in Christ Jesus I have begotten you through the gospel.

If we want to be strictly biblical in our thinking and methods, one has to question the scope of the f/s ministry paradigm for any relationship other than that of a convert and the one who leads him/her to conversion and subsequent growth in the faith. The context of 1 Corinthians 4:15 is explicit and frequently ignored when this topic is preached. Paul's metaphor of spiritual fatherhood is related to birthing in the gospel: conversion, new birth.

Some believe the image is not limited to conversion, but to being "fathered in ministry." Paul simply does not use the metaphor in such a way. It's not in the text. It's a weak, if not illegitimate inference. To categorically adapt this language to a relationship of someone who has transferred from another assembly or who has joined an apostle's "network," is a very dubious application of Scripture.

Joining a network or association no more establishes a f/s relationship than putting a mouse in a cookie jar makes it a cookie. Any organization resembling a "Christian entity" legitimately exists only as a context for the development of relationships of mutuality, not as the source of identity or value.

It's biblically illegitimate to make much of a little. It's one thing to use the language of family, fatherhood, sonship, and children to describe Holy Spirit birthed unique relationships associated with conversion. It's another matter altogether to turn the language into a mandatory and universal spiritual protocol of "ministerial relationship" that all must submit to under dire threats of missing God's best for his or her life.

2. The Limitations of Family # 2 – Cross Pollination

Those who strongly advocate a f/s paradigm commonly teach by analogy that just as in any house or family, there is only one father and one family DNA, so it is in the spiritual family and church: there can only be one legitimate spiritual father (pastor/apostle/leader) in the spiritual family who is the source of spiritual seed/DNA.

This is a classic example of the danger of dogma by analogy, and making too much of too little. It sounds good, rational, and logical. It's utterly unbiblical, as the keystone proof text used by those who advocate for the f/s paradigm quoted above makes clear (1 Cor. 4:15).

The Scripture does **not** say: "You only have one father." Paul implies the limited potential for having fathers (plural) in the faith. An individual may have one or several spiritual fathers! Better none than the wrong one or some artificially contrived relationship that provides a false sense of identity. Ultimately, those who may not have been "fathered" by an apostle or taught by one of the ten thousand guides Paul refers to still have access to The Father of all lights. In God's redemptive economy the actual is never hostage to the ideal.

Contrary to the popular spiritual DNA teaching, spiritual health requires the input of diverse fathers. There's a reason in the natural we don't marry our cousins! Family health requires the input of diverse genetic elements over time!

Paul never claimed singular fatherly authority over the churches in his sphere of ministry. We know he invited others to pollinate the congregations[6] in a fatherly way, taking the chance that carnal loyalties might develop. They did. Paul had a holy jealousy and a watchful eye for those entrusted to him, but this did not manifest in carnal possessiveness. Unlike much, if not the majority of f/s teaching that is prevalent today, Paul was not clingy, proprietary, or parochial in his concept of spiritual fathering and, yes, it cost him. The real thing will cost us also.

It's appropriate that deep relational bonds of affection and oneness might develop with a specific individual that could express itself in father-son type dynamics. However, thinking those bonds translate into a loyalty that forbids the influence of others betrays the Pauline concept of spiritual fatherhood.

3. The Limitations of Family #3 – The NT Household

Another weakness with common presentations of the f/s or single DNA paradigm is that it is not biblically consistent at a cultural level.

---

[6] 1 Corinthians 1:12.

The term for "family" (meaning that which is of paternal lineage) is only used **once** in the NT Epistles[7] and it refers to the human race descended from God as Father! It is **never** used in the Epistles to describe any relationship within the church!

The term used in the NT to describe the family of God is *oikos*. It means "household." In ancient times the household included natural born sons, women/wives, daughters, slaves, and freemen. Singular DNA does not define the "family" or "household" of faith! The NT *oikos* is not limited to just "my sons" who have my DNA!

The promise of the New Covenant is the INCREASE of the household of God, not related to anyone's DNA other than Christ's!

PRAISE GOD!

The limited DNA analogy of apostolic spiritual fatherhood is not new revelation. It is regression. It is error.

4. The Limitations of Family #4 — Divine Boundaries

I have been in more than one faith community where the advocacy for spiritual parenting and spiritual sonship became so strong that it out ranked the God-ordained natural lines of familial authority and affections. That is, "spiritual Moms and Dads" out ranked natural parents in relationship to their children, both legal minors and adults.

For instance, it was taught (in more than one environment) that if one's natural parents (who were believers, faithfully serving God) were not "spiritually mature" or not "discerning" in spiritual matters (how these are measured and who decides them, well, that's another story), that a child's or adolescent's responsibility to obedience should not be to his or her natural parents, but to the spiritual leadership of the organization.

The emerging emotions and affections of young people were manipulated by "spiritual fathers" to alienate the young people from their natural parents and to emotionally bond with the "spiritual

---

[7] Ephesians 3:14-15. It is used in the Gospels to describe natural lineage and the promise of family like relationship for those whose profession of faith cost them their natural relationships (Mark 10:29-30).

parents." Natural parents were excluded from influence in the lives of their own children, even into adulthood.[8]The trauma and suffering caused by this "revelation" is still in effect today in the lives of many who were involved.

5. Disenfranchisement

The indiscriminate application of the f/s model, by design or default, sets up classes of people. It does not facilitate a spirit of family in a community. It separates people into the enfranchised and the disenfranchised—a "Christianized" caste system. The enfranchised are those viewed by the "fathers" as **"their"** sons who are fulfilling their spiritual and moral mandates by their alleged sonship and loyalty. Then there are . . . the rest . . . the "non-sons" . . . Well, it's non-sense.

There's nothing wrong with the development of different degrees of relational intimacy with different people. In fact, it's healthy both psychologically and spiritually to do so. However, that's not the same as strategically building class distinctions into our faith communities through the clumsy implementation of an ill-perceived spiritual concept.

The psychological pressure to conform or to build artificial constructs of sonship in these environments will be **intense** (See 8 below). People without a strong sense of identity will scramble to do whatever they must to be advanced into the "status" of spiritual son, especially if spiritual advancement or gift expression is contingent upon reaching the status of being a spiritual son. Legitimate spiritual sonship is not a status or identity moniker. It is a spiritual reality . . . or it is nothing.

This dynamic of disenfranchisement is so contrary to the truth of the Gospel and so contrary to Paul's word and spirit[9] that the word wicked comes to mind as not too strong an adjective.

---

[8] I am not talking about intervention in cases of legal, moral or substance abuse problems. I am talking about regular folks who, in the eyes of their "leadership" just didn't measure up to the standards of spirituality the leadership thought to be appropriate.

[9] 2 Corinthians 12:15.

In Paul's universe, what of Apollos, Silas, Mark, Demas, Aristarchus, Luke, Stephanas, the list in Romans 16 and others? Paul *never* refers to them as his sons/daughters. Yet he was clearly in relationship with them all, effectively working with them, referring to them as fellow prisoners, helpers, and laborers in the gospel. Sometimes it was a peer relationship and sometimes not.

Were these individuals on the "B team" because of lack of a sonship relationship to Paul? Of course not, and it is an inference to assume that they had to be someone else's spiritual son because "that's God's order of things."

The New Covenant gospel begins with the inclusion of all the previously disenfranchised classes of society (slaves, Gentiles, and women). Under the guise of restored truth or revelation it has become for some a restrictive association of privilege for "sons." Surely, different benefits can accrue through different relationships. But a spirit of exclusivity and elitism is not biblical sonship. Let all who are thirsty . . . come . . . not just "your sons."

6. Recruiting Sons

There is no scriptural example, anywhere, for the concept of recruiting spiritual sons. Recruitment is practiced commonly today as if it is a heaven-sanctioned methodology.

We do not, and should not, preach sonship as a "thing." We preach Christ and him crucified, and if in our preaching Christ, individuals come to the new birth and form the bonds of affection and trust typified by a father-son relationship, that is all well and good. However, it's illegitimate to traverse the countryside preaching sonship when sonship means the recruiting of individuals into the sphere of one's personal influence.

Building a "family" or a "network of sons" from unresolved/unhealed psychological issues is not biblical spiritual fatherhood.

It's true that the Lord sets the fatherless in families—the spiritual can compensate for lack in the natural. This is wonderful and redemptive. However, I've noticed that those who come from very broken family backgrounds can come into a faith community with an inner compulsion to make "family" happen for themselves. Their pursuit of a proverbial father figure/family relationship can be greater than their pursuit of the Lord. Opportunists can, and do, take advantage of this human vulnerability.

What can appear on the surface to be a spirit of fatherhood can easily be nothing other than the enthusiastic overflow of our own unhealed heart—the need to be needed, and the need to be the center of attention, affection, loyalty, and honor. The need to be needed is not spiritual fatherhood, though it can look like it in practice to the undiscerning.

It's also common for those who come from a background of a lack of validation from earthly fathers (natural and spiritual) to latch on to the "message of sonship" and preach it because of the relief it brings them psychologically and socially. It is not a Holy Spirit birthed message even though it may be propped up with chapter and verse.

Merely grabbing, preaching, and implementing the so-called "sonship message" when the need to be needed or other inner life issues, have not been healed, ***inevitably*** results in a spirit of control, not the spirit of fatherhood. Controllers are often blind and self-justifying in their control—some in ignorance, some in malice.

It's common to experience a few controlling false starts during the treasure hunt for genuine relationship with "spiritual parents." The short definition of the difference between control and fatherhood is fatherhood respects, validates, dignifies, honors, develops, and releases individual personhood (including challenge and discipline). Control does the opposite. It restrains, suppresses, dehumanizes, and discourages the expression of individual personhood, often under the guise of submission to spiritual authority and conformity to group norms of behavior. It is a very ugly distortion.[10]

7. False Identity/Titles

The apostolic/prophetic movement is saturated with the language of "I am so and so's spiritual son." In some circles the practice of calling your mentor or spiritual father has grown into the use of titles: Father

---

[10] Please refer to *Authority, Accountability, and the Apostolic Movement* for a deeper discussion.

Jim, Daddy Steve, Dad Richard, Papa Smith, etc. It is believed this custom honors those "over us."

This is usually a somewhat benign attempt at honor, but it misses the mark. There's simply not a single example in the NT of any one using such language. If Matthew 23:9[11] means anything at all, it at least hints that the custom should be avoided if not stopped.[12] Not once are any of the apostles referred to passively by others as "Dad" or "Daddy," or "Father."

The apostolic prohibition against identifying with any individual apostle[13] is crystal clear. The hermeneutical lengths of sophistry individuals will go to evade this stark simplicity is amazing. I have heard it said that Paul prohibits being "of" Apollos or Peter, but he does not prohibit being "from" Apollos or Peter in the sense of spiritual seed or issue. We are the spiritual issue of Christ, not man. We sprang from His loins, not man's. Apparently, I can belong to an apostle as long as I don't act like it.

I know the Scriptures are inspired precisely, but I doubt if the Holy Spirit is as sophisticated with prepositions as we appear to be. Playing with a preposition to avoid the clear, explicit, apostolic ban on practices that we want to do in spite of what the Scriptures say is inexcusable.

Those from a Protestant background would recoil at the Roman practice of entitling their clergy as Father so and so, yet we embrace the same practice in our own spheres and call it new revelation.

I would argue, that any loyalty other than loyalty to Christ is misdirected loyalty. Now, loyalty to Christ can work out in a communion of gift exchange of love and service that benefits all members of the community. This is fine, but being labeled or taking one's identification as a devotee or "son" of Apostle Father so and so, is a mistake.

---

[11] Call no man father.

[12] Please refer to *Authority, Accountability, and the Apostolic Movement* for a deeper discussion.

[13] 1 Corinthians 1:12ff.

"Father" is neither a title nor a pseudo-office of spirituality. It's a spiritual relationship and reality . . . or it is nothing.

8. Psychological Abuse

Consider this hypothetical scenario that's not all that hypothetical! I have seen similar situations happen on multiple occasions.

Imagine I am a mature "father," 50 years old or more with a strong teaching gift, a strong personality, charisma, the flow of spiritual manifestations, and decades of experience. Before me are 150 young people between the ages of 18-30. These young people have various degrees of unhealed psychological issues and identity needs. I preach intensely and passionately for a week to these people about how everyone must have a spiritual father if they are to satisfy God, fulfill their destiny, or be all that God intends for them, and how they will never reach their potential if unconnected to an apostolic father.

What kind of psychological pressure do you think might be on one of these young people (or psychologically fragmented adult "ministers") at the end of the week? What "father" happens to be available at the moment? Who is likely to accrue benefit in this scenario by preaching sonship to the vulnerable under the guise of revelation? Convenient is it not?

Do you think many of the folks in the crowd, especially a young person, would have the courage to stand on their own and resist the teaching from the 50-year-old father/expert and say: "No thank you?" I highly doubt it.

I propose that to deny this psychological phenomenon is to be naïve. To have the lives of others under our power of influence is a sacred thing, not to be presumed upon. If we have a captive audience of immature, psychologically unhealed, and alienated young people, (or lonely "ministers"), looking for identity and belonging, and we pummel them for a week with the importance of sonship, we are operating in a soulish predatory spirit, and a form of psychological manipulation and abuse, regardless of whatever justifying Bible verse we may believe.

PREACH CHRIST! NOT SONSHIP! Present His excellencies and provision in all the power of the Spirit, not the need to be associated with an apostle. Identity and belongingness are found in Him, not in relationship with an apostle! Wonderful human relationships of all sorts may derive from preaching Christ accurately! Legitimate sonship may be a derivative of preaching Christ accurately. But if we preach sonship as the essential, rather than Christ, we will find our selves on the wrong side of the interests of the Lord and His kingdom, even with a proof text on our lips.

9. Inordinate Bonding

This issue relates to another dimension of human psychology. I like to use the phrase "managed expectations." It applies in so many areas of life.

When people with deep need associate themselves with gifted ministers or "spiritual fathers," there can be many unarticulated expectations. It is so critical that all loyalty and alignment be unto Christ, not one another. Relational breakdown occurs when emotional and relational needs are not met. It is error for any minister to set him or her self up as the father/mother to whom subordinate children must rely upon solely to have their needs met.

Inordinate bonding also manifests as a subtle and often unarticulated sense of another person being "mine" in the sense of "my" spiritual son/daughter. Again, this is where the family metaphor breaks down.

Naturally, a child belongs to a set of parents who are solely responsible to meet the needs of the child, but spiritually, that is NOT true. There's only One who has ownership rights and it ain't us! There's only One who's resourced to meet needs sovereignly from heaven and through His Body! A spiritual father or mother is merely part of the company of others designed by God to meet needs through gift exchange.

It's relationally and emotionally addictive to believe that another human being is dependent on you, your insights, and gifts. The greatest favor a spiritual mother or father can do for a new believer is to point out the excellencies of the resources in Christ the Head and

His Body! Teach dependency on the Head and His Body, NOT dependency on ANY individual, including our selves.

Should a genuine spiritual bonding by the Holy Spirit emerge between a father/mother and a son/daughter, it is CRITICAL that expectations be managed. They must be spoken about, openly, early, and explicitly. Individuals can only supply what they have received from Christ. Spiritual demand must be equivalent to the spiritual supply. It is a violation of each other if we do not have these kinds of conversations. I have no right to be offended in interpersonal dynamics if there's not advance mutual agreement to expectations.

If I get offended or hurt by the behaviors of others for which there is no biblical prohibition, it's **my** issue. Failure of others to meet my unarticulated emotional expectations, my self-perceived needs, is **not** sin. However, projecting my own soul damage or unarticulated emotional expectations onto another human being is sin! Allowing my feelings over such things to escalate to the point of relational or community breakdown is sin!

10. Centrality

In atmospheres where f/s methods are practiced it's very common for Jesus to get lost in the house of His friends. That is, the spiritual father, the patriarch, becomes the centrality and the focus of the ministry. All questions must be addressed to the father. All activities must be structured for the father. All honor must go to the father. All submission is due the father. The true essence of spiritual fatherhood is to make oneself insignificant for the benefit of others, not demand, require, or ***illicitly enjoy***, a place of centrality.[14]

Here's a current and true example of how dangerous focusing on the centrality of the "fathers" can be:

Within this past year there was a conference hosted by a self-proclaimed apostle and "spiritual father." This man is of some notoriety, is widely read, the head of an international network and considers himself an apostolic "covering"[15] for his people. In the

---

[14] 2 Corinthians 12:13-15.

[15] I do not believe in the concept. See *Authority, Accountability, and the Apostolic Movement.*

meeting one of his “sons” took the platform to extol the virtues of this “apostolic father.” The son went on and on about how significant this apostolic father had been in “all our lives” and how much we “owe him” - that sort of thing.

Then the young man said something along the lines of: “I believe that we all should show the depth of our alignment to Apostle X by coming forward and being spiritually baptized into Apostle X.” Well, sad to say, 80% of the congregation came forth to be baptized into Apostle X. The other “fathers” on the platform said and did nothing. They went along with it. Fortunately, about 20% of the congregation got up and left the meeting, as they should have.

11. Gift-Projection and Legacy

There’s an issue that I’d like to submit for your consideration.

The individuals who use the language of children/sonship in the Epistles are Paul, Peter, and John. They have something in common. They’re all apostles. There’s no NT evidence that a teacher, or a prophet, or an evangelist used the language of spiritual sons. You can’t make much of an argument from silence, but combined with my subjective experience, it has caused me to wonder about some things.

I suggest that the paradigm of father-son relationship is particularly appropriate for those with an apostolic gift, but that some discretion, and perhaps even reluctance should be exercised in presuming to normalize the dynamic and project that reality on to all the other Ephesians 4 gifts.

It’s often taught (especially by those with an apostolic gift) that unless one is begetting spiritual sons and thereby creating a legacy for one’s self, one’s existence as a minister is barely legitimate and surely failing God’s purpose. It is held that a valid ministry must be able to point to the body count of “sons” at their feet as validation for their ministerial existence.

This sounds good, and is frequently based on extensive Old Covenant typological teaching regarding sons and inheritance. Elijah and Elisha are often used as an example. It is of course legitimate to disciple others, including across generational (f/s) lines. However, using the "my father, my father" of the Elijah/Elisha story as a normative model for the New Covenant is a mistake.

In the Old Covenant economy the anointing rested singularly and solely on individuals. It was a "have and have not" situation. Person A has the anointing, and person B does not. If person B wants the anointing, he/she must receive it through and from person A, just like a person receives literal life from a father. Therefore, if separated from the father, the individual could not receive what the father had, just like without a father, you could not receive life. This is simply no longer true. The New Covenant operates differently.

In the New Covenant the anointing has been released on the day of Pentecost, heaven is open. There are no mediating brokers of the anointing. Everyone ***in Christ has received***, and ***is*** anointed. The "person B's" of the Old Covenant no longer exist. We are all "person A's." We have received directly from The Father, through His Son.

The motif of interdependency from the Old Covenant is maintained in the new era. But what was dependency upon an individual father (Elijah) of the old economy has become the interdependency of the "one anothers" of the New economy. The anointing rests on the Body. The necessity of relating to an Elijah-father of the Old has become the necessity of relating to a Community, a Body, in the New. Mutuality of gift exchange, has replaced dependency on singular anointings.

I know what I am saying will grate on many who come from a Pentecostal and Charismatic background with a strong emphasis on the laying on of hands, impartation, mantle transfer, etc. I just cannot go into it all here. I would recommend the relevant chapters in our book, *Healing: Hope or Hype?*[16] for a detailed discussion regarding mistaken notions concerning the anointing which result from a lack of understanding of the change that has taken place from the Old to the New Covenant.

By the "must have sons" measure neither Christ nor Paul could have justified their ministries. They both died virtually alone and forsaken by the vast majority of those they had given their lives to. Their legacy was realized AFTER their mortal departure, AND it was

---

[16] As well as posted articles on our web page, www.stevecrosby.org.

realized spiritually, not literally. If legacy is a legitimate concept, I believe it must be defined based on death and resurrection, not body count of sons.

Some legacy may be seen. Some legacy may not be seen. In modern times, there have been many who during their mortality could point to nothing resembling spiritual sons. I can think of two individuals in particular in this regard: Oswald Chambers and T. Austin Sparks. Neither had what we would call a ministry accompanied by "sons" and they died relatively unknown. Yet their legacy continues to speak to millions on a scale and scope that could never have been realized during their mortality.

The notion of visible legacy is very appealing, but will not withstand full NT examination, and I would appeal for gift mix and calling sensitivity in this matter. I think the "you must have sons," "no success without a successor" motif is very suspect for a broad spectrum.

12. Government

Another limitation of the f/s paradigm regards church government. It is commonly taught among those who believe in the f/s platform as a standard methodology that only sons are qualified to be elders or leaders in a church environment.

I heard an apostle once say that until someone proves his sonship loyalty for at least 15 years, he/she is not ready to be an elder "under you" (something else I do not believe in!) Of course, this has a certain pretense of wisdom . . . "Oh, yes, we want only mature leaders." But the problem (among many) is that it's simply not biblical. Paul was in Ephesus between 2-3 years and in that time frame, from stump worshipping pagans, he raised up elders, and left them alone knowing they would experience troubles.[17]

Nowhere does the NT say that an elder must be a spiritual son to the pastor/apostle. I would suggest that spiritual health might require a mix of those who have a sonship relationship and those who do not.

The father-son motif as it applies to issues of government is often

---

[17] Acts 20.

rooted in the insecurities of the "senior leader" (Something else I don't believe in . . . getting to be quite a collection!). By establishing this principle, the chances of being hurt or betrayed are minimized. Jesus, who was the Son of sons, did not require that those "under Him" be His "sons." At the command of His Father He chose someone who was a devil and who ultimately would cause Him pain beyond description.

13. Finance

It's commonly taught in the spiritual f/s paradigm that the sons have a duty to "tithe up and out " to the fathers. That is, a minister or local church pastor's tithe must go to his "covering apostle," not the local church as that as viewed as "tithing to yourself" and supposedly your tithe then "doesn't count" (?). It's believed by moral obligation and Scriptural mandate that the "father" is entitled to the tithe of his sons.

This is not the place to digress into discussion about the tithe.[18] However, this teaching invariably leads to a recruiting of spiritual sons mentality, because as the father of the relationship or organization, I am now economically dependent on the support of the children even though, again, this is contrary to Paul in spirit and letter.[19] My financial increase is linked to the number of "sons" under my "covering." It should be obvious that this teaching is just a Christian pyramid scheme.

Meeting the material needs of others, especially of those who teach us, from an attitude of love and a charitable heart is biblically legitimate.[20] However, being told God will curse you if you do not tithe to your covering apostle/father is not.

What Then?

Simplify. Return to basics.

---

[18] For the interested please refer to my own *Wealth Transfer: Tracing Trends in Money and Ministry* or Matthew E. Narramore. *Tithing: Low-Realm, Obsolete, & Defunct*. Graham: Tekoa Publishing, 2004, 15.

[19] 2 Corinthians12:13-14. Children do not lay up for the fathers.

[20] Galatians 6:5-10.

Love God, love your neighbor, love each other as Christ has loved us, is not complicated. It doesn't require a lot of father-son revelation and apostolic-prophetic mechanics. It requires a lot of death and resurrection.

The father-son paradigm is a lot like the relationship of a man and woman in a marriage bond or the marriage bed. It's a beautiful, God-sanctioned thing. But to be talking about it all the time is unbecoming and inappropriate. Talking about it, teaching about it, in no way approximates the reality of the mystery of it, and in many ways can become a counterfeit for it. Those that are enjoying it do not need to validate and vindicate it. You can tell by the glow on their face and the light in their eyes that they have found the real thing.

Inaccuracy has consequences. Let's avoid them.

Father-son terminology is a legitimate limited biblical metaphor describing a precious interpersonal Spirit-born relationship. It is not an institution of ministerial protocol that must be adhered to at all costs that can be shopped for like buying a pair of shoes. It is a quality of relationship, not a limiting format for ministry. Problems will develop when we try to institutionalize, codify, and reproduce an essentially spiritual quality.

Part II

Apostolic and Prophetic Perspectives

Disclaimer

The focus herein on things apostolic and prophetic is not meant to imply any sense of superiority of one ministry gift over another, or of some clergy-laity distinction. In what is already a lengthy piece, I cannot cover every nuance of these issues. From time to time, I will use language that I do not even believe in myself! It's the necessity of the limitations of language and scope of this article.

My own focus on these issues somewhat rubs me the wrong way! In these days I find the incessant drum beat about apostles and prophets to be narcissistic and tiring. In my universe, some of us have been talking about these things for 40-60 years. It's time to just get over our own self-significance and get on with kingdom labors.

A bird that has to constantly talk about itself (I'm a bird, I'm a bird, look everyone, I'm a bird!) and explain itself (I can fly, I can fly!) isn't much of a bird. Just get on with flying. Everyone will know what you are . . . unless they've never seen a bird, or have never had one explained to them. If that's the case, explanation is necessary. What's tiresome for some (including myself) is necessity for others based on the degree of previous exposure.

The Authentic vs. the Counterfeit

A point of view is often put forth that when engaged in kingdom efforts, we should not worry about that which is false, but merely present that which is genuine. The presentation of the genuine supposedly passively neutralizes the influence of the counterfeit. Addressing that which is false is considered to be misdirected effort, a waste of time, or worse, not Christ-like.

In the sense of general wisdom, let the dead bury the dead, before the Judge we all will stand, ignoring the insincere preaching of Christ, etc., I would agree: leave things alone. It's particularly true if ignoring the false means avoiding obsessive faultfinding, heresy hunting, or self-appointed policing of the kingdom. The accurate representation of Christ in word and deed is the best antidote to falsehood. However, the "only present the genuine" perspective is not scripturally sustainable.

1. The OT prophets clearly dealt with that which is false.[21] Paul dealt with that which is false. John dealt with that which is false.[22] The argument could be made that the bulk of the NT epistles are responses to that which is false. Certainly, Colossians and Galatians are cases-in-point. Christ himself dealt directly with His followers concerning that which is false.[23]

2. There are also practical weaknesses of the "only deal with the genuine" paradigm. First, those who traffic in various degrees of falsehood and deceit use it as a defense mechanism to keep themselves and their methodologies from being objectively scrutinized. Secondly, if someone is laboring in "virgin territory" so to speak, "ignore the false" is likely true (Paul ignored Diana of the Ephesians when in Ephesus). But if someone is working in a circumstance of spiritual remodeling, recovery, or reclamation it's often necessary to clear debris before new construction can go forward. It's actually easier to present Christ accurately to a pagan than it is to remodel a Christian or to reclaim a wounded/broken one.

Apostles and Prophets: Partners in Tension

I believe "ignore the false/ go forward" versus "don't go anywhere until you straighten what's crooked," tension is one of the differences between those called apostolically and those called prophetically. It's also a reason why prophets and apostles need each other and work the best in tandem.

The essence of being apostolic or prophetic is more than just ~~expressing a "gift" or an "office" (~~a term which I do not believe in) in a

[21] Myriad examples in the OT.

[22] He that does not confess, etc.

[23] Beware the leaven of the Pharisees is not passive. You have to recognize it and avoid it. "I have somewhat against you . . . is focusing on the negative. These are just two of many examples.

"church meeting" of some sort. They're divinely prescribed interior configurations (Old or New Covenants). Both are unique sets of personality, mental, emotional, and spiritual grids, through which an individual processes both natural and kingdom life.

It has been my subjective observation over the years, that some individuals are not well-equipped or graced to deal with that which is false, broken, or in need of repair (so to speak). It's not a matter of personal deficiency, per se. It's a matter of personality, temperament, and sometimes, divine calling. Everyone has strengths and weaknesses and is one reason among many why we need one another's complimentary gifts! None of us possesses all resources for all situations. The fullness of Christ resides in the Body, no single individual.

Highly focused, hard charging, and "forward thrust" type of individuals can be quite unaware of the struggles and pain of people who happen to be in the wake of their spiritual boat. They can view having to spend excessive time dealing with the weak or broken as a hindrance to the mission, sometimes forgetting that the weak and the broken . . . are the mission and we all are the weak and the broken!

Forward thrust sorts of individuals are often capable of expressing high levels of human care and compassion at a social or inter-relational level. In fact, they are often quite warm and engaging in their personality (which is often mistaken for the operation of a spiritual gift . . . but that is another story!). But when it comes to the "job" . . . forward focus is the mainspring of their lives.

The Scriptures hint that the Apostle Paul may not have been the easiest guy on the planet to get along with. His relentless drive for forward motion and kingdom advance may have left a soul or two in his wake. We can see hints of this in his relationship with John Mark. He seems to have had very little tolerance for weakness that hinders the mission. It seems that Paul mellowed in his later years. John Mark probably matured and Paul probably softened.

Generalizations are just that. There are always exceptions and blends, but when the same phenomenon is repeatedly observed in different places and with different people, one cannot help but begin to connect some subjective dots.

Most, if not all, of the individuals that I have known in the category I am describing have been apostles (some authentic, some not) or those who have some degree of "apostolic wiring" in their make up. It does not mean there's anything wrong with them. They're just incomplete. They cannot but help fulfill their mandate with the gift and perspective they have been given.

Mature prophets,[24] on the other hand, are very concerned about the oppressed, injustice, and making the crooked straight. You cannot read the OT prophets and not see this insight into the psyche and mandate of a prophet. There are differences in application between the OT and NT prophetic, but the prophetic psyche or temperament is, I think, consistent. This also does not mean there's anything wrong with them. They're just incomplete. They cannot but help fulfill their mandate with the gift and perspective they have been given.

In the matter of the f/s teaching and its expression, I've noticed that most apostles want to present the genuine and most prophets want to straighten that which is crooked. Apostles generally believe everything is fine and we should just "get on with it" while discerning prophets are saying . . . stop the train . . . some folks have had enough and want to get off . . .

And speaking of trains . . . [25]

In the early days of steam locomotives passengers had to deal with the soot and cinders spewed by the engine exhaust. Covered passenger cars developed quickly not only to keep the weather out, but also to keep the passengers from catching fire!

After the advent of covered cars, even opening a window meant one took a chance of taking in some soot and occasional hot cinders. Passengers were often covered with the exhaust of the engine. If an individual was riding in the caboose, he or she could see the entire exhaust trail from the engine, and whether or not the passengers were dealing with the necessary, but unpleasant output of the engine

---

[24] Young prophets-"PIT's" (prophets-in-training) are not necessarily so wired. They tend to be flame-throwers and fire bombers.

[25] Every metaphor is limited. I am not implying a disengaged laity along for the ride. I also understand that the prophetic element of sightedness could be viewed as being at the front of the train and prophets put out their share of soot. It's a limited metaphor . . . don't push it too far.

of their forward motion. Dealing with soot was “part of the deal” of riding a train.

Apostles are like the locomotive at the front of the train. Their focus is full steam ahead. They have job to do and all their vision, energy, and drive is to pull the train and arrive at the destination. This is as it should be. They are not interested in what is behind, but what lies ahead. But just like the locomotive, their orientation on the track often prevents them from seeing the incidental impact of their forward energies. They put out soot they are not aware of. Apostolic soot (not limited to just apostles of course, but limited in this metaphor) is not pleasant. It causes pain.

Mature prophets on the other hand are like the caboose of the train. They can see the unintended consequences of what the locomotive is leaving behind. They might even get a face full of soot. They’re not wrong or deficient because they deal with negative consequences of combustion whereas apostles deal with the positive potential of combustion. Apostles and prophets cover both ends of the train! They are both part of the necessary process to get a people to a destination!

Individuals operating on the front end of the train of God’s purposes probably don’t have to deal much with the negative. Individuals operating at the caboose end may do nothing but deal with the negative. Ignoring the negative might be totally appropriate in some spheres and temporarily focusing on it a necessity in others. We all must be careful not to project the specifics of our individual spheres of ministry and calling onto one another.

I would argue, that if the prophets are not allowed to deal with the soot, the time will come when there will be no one on the apostolic train . . .

And speaking of no one . . . [26]

My good friend, Greg Austin, is ex-military, though he would argue that it’s not possible to be ex-military. The man might leave the military, but the military might not leave the man! He shares a military metaphor of the same nature as my train analogy.

---

[26] Again, a limited metaphor, don’t over apply it.

Generals see the big picture and understand the strategies of warfare. Generals accept that there will pain and loss of life involved in achieving an objective. You simply cannot fight a war without sustaining casualties. However, the further removed one is from the rank-and-file soldier in the foxhole, the less aware one is of the conditions being experienced by that soldier.

When you move from general officer down the ranks, through subordinate officers, you come to the non-commissioned officers. Moving from senior to junior, you arrive at the "heart" of the army: the buck sergeants and the sergeants-first-class. These men recently were privates and corporals. They were the "grunts." Now they command others of lesser rank, but unlike the generals, they have personal relationships. They are buddies with the privates.

When an 18-year-old dies before his first shave and his sergeant is covered with what used to be the brains of his best friend, it crushes the sergeant. A general, while caring, asks: "Did we accomplish the mission?" The sergeant has to deal with a dead buddy. The general moves a token on a map. Whose perspective is “right?” It all depends on what one is commissioned to do.

An apostolic missional mandate is like a general’s. But just like the generals need sergeants to keep them in touch with the real cost of the mission, so apostles need prophets to keep them in touch with the real cost of the mission. A general who is indifferent to the perspective of the sergeant will soon be the general or leader of no one . . . the leader of an army of one . . . himself . . . assuming he avoids friendly fire in the back of the head.

Apostles and advocates of the f/s paradigm must admit that there has been extensive collateral damage done in the Body of Christ with the f/s teaching, even if they don't "see it" and are not called to deal with it. Many would admit that they are not graced to see it, and not called to deal with it. That’s why they feel the way they do about it and have no inclination to want to focus on it!

However, prophets, because of their giftedness, more readily see the damage (some of which they have caused) and they **are** called to deal with it! Prophets should not project on apostles and apostles should not make prophets feel like they are doing something wrong by dealing with defects and damage.

For the sake of getting the train to the station and not suffering more casualties than necessary in the battle, we **<u>all</u>** need to know these things:

- our identity (who we are in Christ)
- our empowerment (our gifts - their strengths and limitations)
- our context (geography/locality and relationships)
- our season (Spirit-led rest or activity and stage of life)

Once these are settled, we can then begin the real work of actually getting along and cooperating with each other in our differences and contributing to something of kingdom significance.

Additional copies of this booklet as well as any of Dr. Crosby's other books, are available on Amazon in soft cover and Kindle formats. PDF, MP3's, and videos are available at stephencrosby.soarlms.com. Please visit our blog at: www.stevecrosby.org.

www.ingramcontent.com/pod-product-compliance
Ingram Content Group UK Ltd.
Pitfield, Milton Keynes, MK11 3LW, UK
UKHW022008190726
13853UKWH00004B/1799

9 798764 578682